Yesterday the HOLY LAND

Yesterday the HOLY LAND

David Roberts

ZONDERVAN PUBLISHING HOUSE
OF THE ZONDERVAN CORPORATION
GRAND RAPIDS, MICHIGAN 49506

Library of Congress Cataloging in Publication Data

Roberts, David, 1796–1864.
  Yesterday the Holy Land.

  David Roberts' illustrations from: The Holy Land, Syria, Idumea,
Arabia, Egypt & Nubia / George Croly. London : F.G. Moon, 1842–
1849; with new text which is translated from the Dutch.
  1. Roberts, David, 1796--1864.   2. Near East in art.
I. Croly, George, 1780--1860. Holy Land, Syria, Idumea, Arabia,
Egypt & Nubia.   II. Title.
NC978.5.R58A4   1982   769.92′4   82-13595
ISBN 0-310-45620-7

Translated by Ed van der Maas
Edited by Edward Viening
Designed by Art Jacobs

Printed in the United States of America

THE LIFE AND WORK OF DAVID ROBERTS

Who was the master who made this series of consummate drawings? His name has been virtually forgotten, although some other names, like Turner and Stanfield, from the Victorian romantic school still are known. But in his day David Roberts was as famous, if not more so, than they. The Scottish artist was known in all of England, but also in Europe and the United States. He traveled and sketched through his own Scotland, through England, throughout Europe (Florence, Rome, Milan, Venice, Livorno, Pisa, Naples, Genoa, Vienna, Prague, Graz, Seville, Cordova, Granada, took a brief trip to Tangiers, and visited Antwerp, Brussels, Bruges, and Gent). He toured like a pilgrim all places of beauty and art, and concentrated especially on architecture. He considered Bruges "the most interesting of all old cities, so entirely different from all other cathedral-cities that I would almost be inclined to be converted to the papacy." He enjoyed so intensely everything he saw and drew, that he saw again and again "the most beautiful city" and "the most beautiful building."

David Roberts (1796–1864) was born into the family of a cobbler. For a while he was a house painter, and later worked as a scene painter for a circus. In the meantime he taught himself to draw and paint. His talent was unmistakable and developed rapidly and well. Recognition came, and he became a member of the Royal Academy, a distinction that was always indicated by the initials "RA" after his name as was customary in those days. He was a friend of Charles Dickens and moved in all cultural circles.

The high point of Roberts' life and work was his long journey through the Near East in 1838 and 1839. He was 42 years old when he left on his expedition. We know from his diaries how many dangers and how much privation he endured, and how the heat and vermin bothered him. Once they had to sink the ship on which they traveled the Nile in order to get rid of the rats! Once a donkey was torn to pieces by a hyena before his eyes. One night his tent was washed away by a torrential downpour. But he could also enjoy himself, especially the sunrises and sunsets, which he called "the most glorious in the world." Sometimes he would also enjoy a Turkish bath. He had quite a bit of trouble with those who accompanied him, such as the hundred Bedouins who accompanied him from Egypt to Aqaba, across the Sinai desert, and the Arabs who, with an entire caravan, went with him from Aqaba to Petra. Language problems often made communication very difficult. In Cairo Roberts disguised himself as an Arab to be able to sketch the Muslim sanctuaries. But from the beginning until the end of the journey he was inspired (or even obsessed) by his work. Indefatigably he sketched the buildings of antiquity. His accomplishment is formidable, even by our contemporary standards. He came home with three hundred sketches, so precise and detailed that he could work them out in a short time in his studio at home. Today Egyptologists and art historians praise the accuracy with which he recorded even architectonic details and sculptures. His work is also valuable for our knowledge of the monuments and landscapes in the nineteenth century.

The drawings of Egypt and the Holy Land were published between 1842 and 1849 in six magnificent folio-sized volumes. The lithographs were prepared by the Belgian, Louis Haghe. For the deluxe edition the plates were colored by hand. It is not known how many copies of the deluxe edition were published. The plates in this volume are from this deluxe edition, acquired with great difficulty volume by volume. The first two editions consisted of 600 copies total. Three smaller but complete editions were published between 1855 and 1858. And this edition of Roberts' drawings of the lands of the Bible will enable many to enjoy once again the romantic beauty of these masterpieces. David Roberts, the forgotten artist, has returned!

Sipke van der Land

1 THE CITADEL OF SIDON

Here we see the remnants of a castle that was built by the crusaders on a small rock island off the coast. Originally it was connected with the mainland by the arches visible in the drawing; today they have unfortunately been replaced by straight walls. What is still standing is much less impressive. The large round tower on the left and the small dome in the center are the only ruins still standing, along with some low walls. The city contains a number of mosques and is inhabited almost exclusively by Muslims.

According to Josephus the city was named after Sidon, the firstborn son of Canaan, one of the sons of Ham. If this is correct, then the city goes back to the period immediately after the Flood. It is still a very ancient settlement with a rich past.

The sons of Ham: Cush, Mizraim, Put and Canaan. Canaan was the father of Sidon his firstborn.
—Genesis 10:6, 15

Citadel of Sidon. March 28th 1839.

David Roberts R.A.

2 ARRIVAL AT NABLUS

The name Nablus is the Arabic corruption of the name the Romans gave this city: Neopolis, "the new city." In the Old Testament it was called Shechem, and in the New Testament Sychar. During the Israelite conquest of Canaan Joshua came here with the tribes of Israel. Later it became the capital of Ephraim. Nablus is now the "capital" of the West Bank.

When Roberts saw it he wrote: "The entire valley was full of gardens and green, and orchards with all kinds of fruits, irrigated by several springs that well up in various places and that flow in refreshing streams westward."

Abram traveled through the land as far as the site of the great tree of Moreh at Shechem. The Canaanites were then in the land, but the LORD appeared to Abram and said, "To your offspring I will give this land."
—Genesis 12:6–7

3 WANDERERS OF THE DESERT

These wanderers of the desert live today much as they did thousands of years ago. They wander with their flocks and pitch their tents wherever they want. They live close to nature and have their own customs and laws. A scene such as this calls to mind the stories of the patriarchs. It reminds us of Abraham, who crossed the desert, traveling at least 600 miles with all his possessions, with his large familes and large flocks, from Mesopotamia to Canaan. And from there God called him to a large task, a great future.

The LORD appeared to Abram and said, "To your offspring I will give this land." So he built an altar there to the LORD, who had appeared to him. From there he went on toward the hills east of Bethel and pitched his tent, with Bethel on the west and Ai on the east. There he built an altar to the LORD and called on the name of the LORD. Then Abram set out and continued toward the Negev.

—Genesis 12:7–9

Mount Seir Wady el Ghor March 4th 1839. David Roberts R.A.

4 HEBRON

Hebron, one of the oldest cities of the world, is the city where the three great patriarchs—Abraham, Isaac, and Jacob—had lived, and where all three were buried in the cave of Machpelah. Across from this cave stands a mosque, its walls covered with texts from the Koran that glorify Abraham. We see many trees in the landscape, and somewhere among them is also the "oak of Abraham" under which the patriarch set up his tent. History makes it clear that Joshua also spent time here, that David reigned here for more than seven years as king of Judah before he became king of the whole nation, and that Absalom began the revolt against his father here. But it is above all else the city of the patriarchs, historically and literally.

So Abram moved his tents and went to live near the great trees of Mamre at Hebron, where he built an altar to the LORD.

—Genesis 13:18

5 THE OMAR MOSQUE IN JERUSALEM

For many centuries the city of Jerusalem has been dominated by the dome of the Mosque of Omar. The octagonal structure (177 feet high and 72 feet in diameter) was built in the seventh century by Kalif Omar. Around 1100 the crusaders made it into a Christian church, but under Saladin (ca. 1190) it again became a mosque.

The mosque stands on Mount Moriah where Abraham almost offered his son Isaac. Inside the mosque is a rock, surrounded by a fence, where this is supposed to have happened. Hence its other name, Dome of the Rock. In the foreground we see Greek Christians praying, facing the sepulcher of Jesus in Jerusalem. They are on the roof of the Church of St. Anna. In the courtyard of the church, which dates from the time of the Crusades, is an ancient bath, probably Bethesda, that can also be seen in this drawing.

Then God said, "Take your son, your only son Isaac, whom you love, and go to the region of Moriah. Sacrifice him there as a burnt offering on one of the mountains I will tell you about."
—Genesis 22:2

AT THE WELL IN NAZARETH

"The figures have all been drawn as they were, and are an accurate representation of the female costume in Nazareth. They wear gold and silver ornaments that contrast beautifully with their black hair, and they present a remarkably graceful appearance to the European eye. The younger women were generally remarkably beautiful, and when they discovered that the strangers were Christians they no longer veiled their faces."

Nazareth was built near a well, and because there was only one well Mary undoubtedly came here to get water; hence the name "well of the Virgin Mary." The well now lies alongside the road to Tiberias. You can still see such picturesque scenes when the beautiful women with pottery jars on their heads come to draw water here toward evening.

He had the camels kneel down near the well outside the town; it was toward evening, the time the women go out to draw water.
—Genesis 24:11

Fountain of the Virgin, Nazareth, April 21st 1839

7 THE GATE OF HEAVEN

Here we are 7362 feet above sea level, and 2345 feet above the St. Catherine monastery. In the side of the mountain 3750 steps have been cut out, and it is said that the monks did this long ago by way of penance. The steps lead to a small gate called "the Gate of Heaven."

Years ago something unusual would take place at the entrance. When a monk and a group of pilgrims would reach this place, the monk would kneel down and pray, after which he would hear the confession of each of the climbers. Anyone who refused was not admitted to the top. This may be the reason why the Egyptian authorities in the nineteenth century constructed another route, much longer but also much easier, that could be traveled by donkey or camel.

When Jacob awoke from his sleep, he thought, "Surely the LORD is in this place, and I was not aware of it." He was afraid and said, "How awesome is this place! This is none other than the house of God; this is the gate of heaven."
—Genesis 28:16–17

Ascent to the Summit of Sinai. Feby 18th 1839

David Roberts R.A.

8

THE GLORY THAT WAS RAMESES

Here lies the colossal torso of a statue that originally stood 56 feet high and weighed more than 1,000 tons. It's hard to believe the ancient Egyptians could have made something like this. This pharaoh lived to be about 90, and during his reign (ca. 1301–1234 B.C.) he built many great structures. The city Rameses, named after him, is known from the Book of Exodus as one of the store cities the Hebrew slaves had to build in the Nile Delta. Other people were also used as slaves by this harsh pharaoh and many had to literally work themselves to death. Now you see here the remnants of the glory of this ruler and you think of thousands of human lives that were sacrificed for it.

So they put slave masters over them to oppress them with forced labor, and they build Pithom and Rameses as store cities for Pharaoh. But the more they were oppressed the more they multiplied and spread; so the Egyptians came to dread the Israelites and worked them ruthlessly.
—Exodus 1:11–12

9

PYRAMIDS BY THE NILE

Five thousand years ago enormous events took place here on the bank of the Nile. The pyramids you see were built in Gizeh, a few miles from the present Cairo. The pyramid on the right consists of 2,000,000 blocks of stone, each weighing 5500 pounds. All the blocks were cut out of the mountains on this side of the river and were transported across on rafts. Someone once calculated that 100,000 slaves worked on this pyramid for about 20 years.

Once papyrus reeds (from which we get our word "paper") covered the banks of the Nile but these reeds are no longer there. It is now difficult to visualize here a small basket, floating among the reeds, with a baby boy in it; Moses, the future viceroy of Egypt, but also the future leader of the delivered nation of slaves.

But when she could hide [Moses] no longer, she got a papyrus basket for him and coated it with tar and pitch. Then she placed the child in it and put it among the reeds along the bank of the Nile.

—Exodus 2:3

Pyramids of Geezeh, from Geezeh.

INSIDE THE MONASTERY

The St. Catherine monastery is built on the spot where, the monks claim, the burning bush once stood. These monks call themselves therefore "the guardians of the burning bush"—the bushes grew from the seeds of the miraculous phenomenon Moses saw. The story is well-known. The Hebrew-Christian prince Moses could not endure to witness the slavery of his own people; he killed an Egyptian slave master, fled to Midian, and saw a burning bush that did not burn up. He also heard the voice of God who called Him.

When entering the Chapel of the Burning Bush you must remove your shoes, as Moses was told to do, "for the place where you are standing is holy ground." Under the altar do not lie the relics of saints, as is usually the case, but the roots of the bush, and the monks claim that this is unique in the Sinai Peninsula.

The angel of the LORD appeared to Moses in flames of fire from within a bush. Moses saw that though the bush was on fire it did not burn up. "Do not come any closer," God said. "Take off your sandals, for the place where you are standing is holy ground."

—Exodus 3:2, 5

11   PHARAOH RAMESES THE GREAT

Many tourists brave the heat to see this spectacle in Abu Simbel, on the west bank of the Nile, in the southern province of Aswan. The statues are more than 65 feet high and, like the temple hidden behind them, are hewn from the sandstone of the cliffs along the banks of the Nile. The chambers in the interior contain beautiful reliefs in color that depict important events in the life of Rameses II, who is usually called "the pharaoh of the Exodus," the man who finally was forced to free the Hebrew people, the nation of slaves. All four statues represent Rameses II, in official ornamental dress, with the double crown on the head. At his feet stand statues of women, representing his wives and daughters.

Pharaoh summoned Moses and Aaron and said, "Up! Leave my people, you and the Israelites! Go, worship the Lord as you have requested. Take your flocks and herds, as you have said, and go."
—Exodus 12:31

SPRINGS AND OASES

It will probably always remain an open question as to which route the Hebrews took when they left Egypt. We do know they crossed a body of water called the "Sea of Reeds" or the "Red Sea."

Here we see the "Springs of Moses" as the local population calls this place, east of the Gulf of Suez, near the coast. In Roberts' day there were about 20 palm trees and some 10 springs. But now "Aioen Musa" as it is called in Arabic, is a large and luxuriant oasis with hundreds of palm trees and numerous springs. This picture reminds us of springs like Elim where the thirst of millions has been quenched through the years.

Then Moses led Israel from the Red Sea and they went into the Desert of Shur. For three days they traveled in the desert without finding water. Then they came to Elim, where there were twelve springs and seventy palm trees, and they camped there near the water.

—Exodus 15:22, 27

13

THE ROCK OF MOSES

Such a remarkable rock formation was bound to lead to the formation of legends. And the well-known story of Exodus 17, with its trenchant style, was a natural starting point.

The whole Israelite community set out from the Desert of Sin, traveling from place to place as the Lord commanded. They camped at Rephidim, but there was no water for the people to drink. So they quarreled with Moses and said, "Give us water to drink." Moses replied, "Why do you quarrel with me? Why do you put the LORD to the test?" But the people were thirsty for water there, and they grumbled against Moses. They said, "Why did you bring us up out of Egypt to make us and our children and livestock die of thirst?" Then Moses cried out to the LORD, "What am I to do with these people? They are almost ready to stone me." The LORD answered Moses, "Walk on ahead of the people. Take with you some of the elders of Israel and take in your hand the staff with which you struck the Nile, and go. I will stand there before you by the rock at Horeb. Strike the rock, and water will come out of it for the people to drink." So Moses did this in the sight of the elders of Israel. And he called the place Massah and Meribah because the Israelites quarreled and because they tested the LORD saying, "Is the LORD among us or not?"

—Exodus 17:1–7

Bedouins have for years pitched their tents in the rugged mountains of the Sinai, and it seems almost impossible that man and beast can live in these rugged circumstances. But these nomads knew the possibilities and impossibilities, and the grandeur of this landscape. And they have always been satisfied with a meager and free existence.

The nomads wandered through the desert when David Roberts painted his pictures, just as did the liberated nation of Israel. How little has changed during all these centuries. In biblical times this was the land of the Amalekites, bitter enemies of the Israelites. Think of the battle Joshua and his men had to fight against them, in which Moses' upraised arms ensured Israel's strength so that by sunset the victory "with the sword" was a reality.

So Joshua fought the Amalekites as Moses had ordered, and Moses, Aaron and Hur went to the top of the hill. As long as Moses held up his hands, the Israelites were winning, but whenever he lowered his hands, the Amalekites were winning. When Moses' hands grew tired, they took a stone and put it under him and he sat on it. Aaron and Hur held his hands up—one on one side, one on the other—so that his hands remained steady till sunset. So Joshua overcame the Amalekite army with the sword.
—Exodus 17:10—13

15

AT THE FOOT OF MOUNT HOREB

This is Mount Horeb, or Mount Sinai, or the Mountain of Moses (the Arabs call it Djibel Musa). The steep, forbidding peaks rise up in front of you, and you realize why Israel spoke of "the Mountain of God." Here Moses received the Ten Commandments, the everlasting rules for a responsible life in harmony with God and fellowman. Given 33 centuries ago, they are still relevant. Moses spent 40 hot days and 40 cold nights on the mountain according to the Book of Exodus, but he came down from the mountain radiant with joy, carrying the two stone tablets inscribed with the commandments. The commandments had already been broken before the law could be given to the people. Yet the laws were given for those people, for all people; for that time, for all time.

The LORD descended to the top of Mount Sinai and called Moses to the top of the mountain. So Moses went up. . . . Moses turned and went down the mountain with the two tablets of the Testimony in his hands. They were inscribed on both sides, front and back. The tablets were the work of God; the writing was the writing of God, engraved on the tablets.

—Exodus 19:20; 32:15—16

Steep trails lead to the top of Mount Sinai. Here we see a small caravan on one of the least steep paths. The artist who recorded this scene for us was deeply impressed by the sunrises and sunsets in these mountains. And not only he. Today small groups of tourists go up the mountain early in the morning before daybreak armed with flashlights, to watch the sunrise. It is an unforgettable experience when the tender light awakes over these astounding mountain peaks, and when you stand there between heaven and earth. It is almost unreal; surrounded by the time and space of all centuries. You think of Moses here who met his God in a very personal manner, under very special circumstances. The giving of the Ten Commandments has given this Sinai an eternal significance for mankind of every age.

When the people saw the thunder and lightning and heard the trumpet and saw the mountain in smoke, they trembled with fear. They stayed at a distance, and said to Moses, "Speak to us yourself and we will listen. But do not have God speak to us or we will die." Moses said to the people, "Do not be afraid. God has come to test you, so that the fear of God will be with you to keep you from sinning."
—Exodus 20:18–20

Desert of the Tomb, passage of Sinai

17 AARON'S GRAVE

The entire company had arrived at Aaron's grave, but they apparently had soon seen all there was to see. Most of them probably did not even enter, because one could only enter barefoot, and "that is not easy in a place where scorpions and snakes like to sit," Roberts says. He adds that the grave is revered by Christians and "even" by Muslims. In agreement with the Book of Numbers, the grave is located on Mount Hor, the Jebel Neby Harun or the Mountain of the prophet Aaron, as the Arabs call it. This mountain rises 4800 feet above the Araba, near the ancient city of Petra in the region of Edom.

And when the whole community learned that Aaron had died, the entire house of Israel mourned for him thirty days.
—Numbers 20:29

David Roberts R.A.

Tomb of AARON, Summit of Mount Hor, March 11th 1839

18 BETWEEN EBAL AND GERIZIM

Nablus lies before us, the city where the Samaritans have continued to live throughout the centuries. They are the direct descendants of the population that came here after the northern kingdom of Israel had been taken into captivity by the Assyrians, and the few who remained mixed here with other peoples. They hold only to the first five books of the Bible, the books of Moses. Their laws are strict and they are forbidden to marry outside their own community.

On the right we see Mount Ebal, the mountain of "cursing." On the left is Mount Gerizim, the mountain of "blessing." Thus the city lies between curse and blessing. On Mount Gerizim the Samaritans had their own temple because they did not want to have anything to do with Jerusalem. The temple was destroyed in 129 B.C.

See, I am setting before you today a blessing and a curse. When the LORD your God has brought you into the land you are entering to possess, you are to proclaim on Mount Gerizim the blessings, and on Mount Ebal the curses.
—Deuteronomy 11:26, 29

Entrance to Nablous   April 17th 1839

"Through the tent opening I watched the glow of the many lamps by the many tents and I was amazed at the different beliefs of the people who congregated here to visit places so dear to the Christians. Many came from the far corners of the Russian empire, and close to me sits a group of black Abyssinians with their blue turbans.

"Shortly before two in the morning the whole multitude was awakened, and at three a rifle gave the sign for departure. The governor sat on his horse and we departed. We followed close behind him. Lights were carried ahead of the governor. The moon was occasionally darkened by black clouds. We traveled in silence and the heavy tread of the whole mass was the only sound that broke the silence of the desert. The day began to break slowly, and this made the scene even more fascinating."

Then Joshua said, "Go, look over the land, especially Jericho."
—Joshua 2:1

20 THE GRAVE OF JOSEPH

Carefully some of the artist's companions approach the tomb of Joseph. Superstitious fear of spirits? This place is near the well of Jacob at Shechem, since in the previous picture we see the tomb in the background. The tomb itself is the rounded piece of stone, and at the head and foot of the grave we see two altars, which the guides in Roberts' day claimed were the graves of Ephraim and Manasseh, the sons of Joseph. Jews, Samaritans, Christians, and Muslims affirm that the grave of Joseph is located here.

And Joseph's bones, which the Israelites had brought up from Egypt, were buried at Shechem in the tract of land that Jacob bought for a hundred pieces of silver from the sons of Hamor, the father of Shechem.
—Joshua 24:32

Tomb of Joseph at Shechem.

David Roberts R.A. 1839

In this drawing we see two regiments of the Egyptian light cavalry on the ancient coastal road near Gaza. It was the most powerful of the five cities of the Philistines. Gaza is known especially from the stories concerning Samson, the judge, who was blinded and imprisoned here, and who died here. The temple of Dagon became a mass grave when this once exceptionally strong man regained his strength for one last time and pulled down the pillars of the temple so it collapsed.

To the right we see a building with domes that indicates the place where Samson is supposed to have put the city gates of Gaza after lifting them from their hinges. The building no longer exists, but this spot is still pointed out as the place where it may have happened.

Then Samson reached toward the two central pillars on which the temple stood. Bracing himself against them, his right hand on the one and his left hand on the other, Samson said, "Let me die with the Philistines!" Then he pushed with all his might, and down came the temple on the rulers and all the people in it.

—Judges 16:29—30

SHEPHERDS NEAR ASHDOD

The ancient and the modern Ashdod lie a little more than 24 miles south of Tel Aviv, not far from the coast, as the drawing shows. Ashdod was part of the five-city league of the Philistines, and was an important religious center because a temple dedicated to their chief god, Dagon, stood there. The story is well-known how the ark of God was captured by the Philistines and placed in the temple in Ashdod next to the statue of Dagon. The next morning Dagon had fallen before the ark, and the same thing happened again the following morning. The ark brought disaster in Gad and Ekron, so that it was finally returned to Israel after seven months.

The modern city of Ashdod was established in 1957 and already has 40,000 inhabitants. After Haifa it is the largest port; it lies south of the ancient city, approximately on the spot of this pastoral scene of shepherds along the coast.

After the Philistines had captured the ark of God, they took it from Ebenezer to Ashdod. The LORD's hand was heavy upon the people of Ashdod and its vicinity. So they moved the ark of the God of Israel.
—1 Samuel 5:1, 6, 8

Ashdod — March 24 1839   David Roberts R.A.

A small stream originates some 650 feet above the water level of the Dead Sea. And thus a delightful oasis is born in the desert of Judah on the shore of the Dead Sea. Clear waterfalls splash down in a narrow strip of abundant vegetation.

The Bible speaks of the "strongholds of En Gedi" as the place where David lived with a small army of exiles when he had to flee from King Saul. It was a safe distance from Jerusalem in the inaccessible mountains, yet near running water in a fertile region. But the king pursued him even here. David had an opportunity to kill Saul in a cave but did not do it out of respect for God's anointed.

After Saul returned from pursuing the Philistines, he was told, "David is in the Desert of En Gedi." So Saul took three thousand chosen men from all Israel and set out to look for David and his men."

—1 Samuel 24:1–2

Convent of S Saba. April 1839

24 ABSALOM'S MONUMENT

In the valley between Jerusalem and the Mount of Olives stands a well-known landmark. Its curious shape and its location make it conspicuous from every direction. From a distance it looks like a small tower, but the relative size of the people in this drawing shows that it is a rather large monument; 59 feet high. It is a sepulchral monument with a chamber in the center. For many years Jews, Christians, and Muslims would bring their unruly sons here to give them a spanking and say to them, "Look, this will happen to you if you don't straighten out your life!" Absalom thus served as a bad example. The memorial is a reminder of this prince who once built a monument to himself and who came to a tragic end because of his disobedience and pride.

During his lifetime Absalom had taken a pillar and erected it in the King's Valley as a monument to himself, for he thought, "I have no son to carry on the memory of my name." He named the pillar after himself, and it is called Absalom's Monument to this day.
—2 Samuel 18:18

Absalom's Pillar.
Valley of Jehoshaphat

25 SAMARIA

Herod called Samaria, Sebaste, in honor of Emperor Augustus, whose Greek name was Sebastos. The Arabic village next to the ruins is still called Sebastya. The Israelis refer to it as Shomron, which means "watchtower," because it was a city with walls and towers. The name Samaria is derived from Semer, the owner from whom King Omri bought the mountain in order to establish a city and a fortress on this strategically located point. For two centuries (until 722 B.C.) it was the capital of the northern kingdom, the ten tribes of Israel. During that time it was a center of idolatry, so that it was continuously warned by the prophets, such as Elijah and Amos, and finally perished in the Assyrian Captivity.

We now find here impressive ruins from various periods: a Roman theater from the first century; a round tower from the Hellenistic period; an Israelite city wall from approximately 750 B.C.; and the "ivory" palaces of Ahab where excess, depravity, and injustice reigned.

Ahab set up an altar for Baal in the temple of Baal that he built in Samaria. Ahab also made an Asherah pole and did more to provoke the LORD, the God of Israel, to anger than did all the kings of Israel before him.

—1 Kings 16:32–33

"The climate is extremely hot and especially unhealthy for strangers," Roberts sighed when he was in Jericho. In his day it was a "miserable village," but today it is a city of 10,000. The ancient biblical city had "disappeared completely, save for a few foundations of city walls." In the center of the drawing a Saracen tower is visible, and to the left the ruins of a Christian church. Somewhere in the area lay the ancient Jericho, the oldest walled city in the world. It was discovered that the city wall was built on the body of the king's oldest son, and the tower on the body of his youngest son. In this manner the king demonstrated that he was willing to sacrifice even his own children to the gods. Yet the invincible walls of Jericho fell when the people of Israel entered the Promised Land here and conquered their first city, wonderfully led by a mighty hand.

In Ahab's time, Hiel of Bethel rebuilt Jericho. He laid its foundations at the cost of his firstborn son Abiram, and he set up its gates at the cost of his youngest son Segub, in accordance with the word of the LORD spoken by Joshua son of Nun.
—1 Kings 16:34

27 MOUNT CARMEL

Mount Carmel has always been known as a beautiful mount, not only because of its shape, but also because so much rain fell on it that it had many vineyards. The name means "vineyard of God." Mount Carmel is known especially because of the contest between the prophet Elijah and the priests of Baal, from which Elijah emerged victorious and which put an end to the worship of Baal. Because of this Elijah had to flee the pagan Queen Jezebel and one of the places he went to was these mountains, which provided a good hiding place with their many caves. At the foot of this mountain now lies Haifa, the second largest city of Israel with a population of more than 200,000.

So Ahab sent word throughout all Israel and assembled the prophets on Mount Carmel. Elijah went before the people and said, "How long will you waver between two opinions? If the LORD is God, follow him; but if Baal is God, follow him."
—1 Kings 18:20–21

28

THE CHAPEL OF ELIJAH

Pious people have always tried to localize the stories of biblical history as much as possible. They have done this with the prophet Elijah, to whom the chapel in this drawing is dedicated. Elijah had to flee from King Ahab of the northern kingdom and from his notorious wife, Queen Jezebel, and the prophet went dejectedly into the desert. But he traveled 40 days and 40 nights to the Mountain of God, Horeb. There he spent the night in a cave and there God appeared to him. Although the mountains are full of caves and caverns, the cave behind the chapel, to the left, is pointed out as the historical place where Elijah stayed. Here God appeared to the prophet and gave him new instructions and new courage.

Then a great and powerful wind tore the mountains apart and shattered the rocks before the LORD, but the LORD was not in the wind. After the wind there was an earthquake, but the LORD was not in the earthquake. After the earthquake came a fire, but the LORD was not in the fire. And after the fire came a gentle whisper. When Elijah heard it, he pulled his cloak over his face and went out and stood at the mouth of the cave.

—1 Kings 19:11b–13

Chapel of Elijah on Mount Horeb. Feby 20th 1839

29

THE HISTORICAL CITY OF JAFFA

Jaffa, Joppa, Jafo—these are some of the names of the historical city that we see here in full glory and beauty from the north. But in 1909 Tel Aviv was built directly next to it, which at present has more than 400,000 inhabitants and is the largest city in Israel. The harbor of Jaffa is one of the most ancient in the world. We know that King Solomon imported the cedar wood from Lebanon via this port, which was the port of Jerusalem, and in the New Testament the city is also mentioned a number of times. Years ago most immigrants entered Palestine via Jaffa, the most important port of entry into the country.

We see how the city is built on a hill. Its location provides a beautiful view of the Mediterranean and of Tel Aviv. On the left is the sandy plain that stretches out for many miles but has now been transformed into Tel Aviv.

Hiram king of Tyre replied by letter to Solomon: ". . . and we will cut all the logs from Lebanon that you need and will float them in rafts by sea to Joppa. You can then take them up to Jerusalem."
—2 Chronicles 2:11, 16

30 JOB'S SPRING

The Valley of Hinnom lies at the foot of the temple mount and stretches to the Kidron Valley. In the time of the Canaanites it was a site of depravity and idolatry, and the Bible says that the pagan priests even sacrificed children here. For unknown reasons a spring in this valley was named for Job, the patriarchal figure from the book that bears his name. The biblical Book of Job poses the question of the meaning of human suffering. He suffered greatly himself and went through a valley of despair, but came out of it through repentance, confession, and grace. Thus the Book of Job is a source of comfort and victory, as refreshing as this spring in the dark valley of depravity, Hinnom.

Though he slay me, yet will I hope in him. The LORD gave and the LORD has taken away; may the name of the LORD be praised.

—Job 13:15; 1:21

Fountain of Job. Valley of Hinnom.

The monastery library, the oldest library in the world, contains a collection of manuscripts of inestimable value, in Greek, Slavic, Arabic, Georgian, etc. In 1844 the German scholar Tischendorf discovered here the "Codex Sinaiticus," a fourth-century translation of the Bible. The codex was centuries older than the oldest then-known manuscript, and a study of this translation shows that even in those early centuries nothing was changed in the copying of the manuscripts of the Bible. The monks show a written statement from Tischendorf promising to return the manuscript, but it now rests in the British Museum in London. Besides such valuable manuscripts the library also contains 5,000 printed books, many of which are among the first ever printed. The gallery of icons contains at least 2,000 of these sacred works of art from all periods of the history of this art form. The oldest icons date from the sixth century, but most are from the eleventh to fifteenth centuries, the golden era of iconography. At certain hours visitors can view about a hundred of these icons.

Send out your light and your truth, let them guide me; let them bring me to your holy mountain, to the place where you dwell.

—Psalm 43:3

In the foreground we see a caravan of Christian pilgrims, as the artist encountered them there, resting in the middle of the day on their way back from Damascus to Jerusalem. Mount Tabor lies 5 miles from Nazareth in the northeastern corner of the valley of Jezreel. The mountain can be seen from a great distance, and its top reaches 1429 feet above sea level. The panorama from here is fascinating: you can see all of Galilee and also the Sea of Tiberias.

According to Byzantine tradition, this was the Mount of Transfiguration, although the New Testament does not say so. Since 1924 a large modern Latin church stands atop Mount Tabor, the "Church of the Transfiguration."

The heavens are yours, and yours also the earth; you founded the world and all that is in it. You created the north and the south; Tabor and Hermon sing for joy at your name.

—Psalm 89:11–12

Mount Tabor from the Plain of Esdraelon
April 17th 1839.

David Roberts. R.A.

33

CHAPELS AND STORIES

The view from the top of the Mountain of Moses is truly breathtaking. David Roberts says that he could see part of the Gulf of Aqaba from here. In his day two small chapels stood on the top, as we can see here, a Christian chapel on the right, and a Muslim one on the left. Both sanctuaries were similar in construction standing side by side as brothers, but both were "very run down due to neglect and the high winds to which they were exposed." They finally collapsed, and in 1934 a new chapel was built using some of the stones from the church that was built there by Emperor Justinian in 532, and that was damaged many times through the centuries.

May the glory of the LORD *endure forever; may the* LORD *rejoice in his works. He looks at the earth, and it trembles; he touches the mountains, and they smoke.*

—Psalm 104:31–32

Convent & Mahomedan Chapels on the Summit of Sinai   Feby 20th 1839.   David Roberts. R.A

34

THE OLD POOL OF SILOAM

In the Kidron Valley we find not only the spring Gihon, but also a pool to which part of its water flowed. A wall was built there to retain and collect the water. The site is now called Birket-el-hamra ("the red pool") and is dry. It is perhaps the "Old Pool" referred to in Isaiah 22 in the oracle concerning Jerusalem's wantonness.

In the upper left we see a section of the city wall. Where we see houses built against the hillside there are no longer any buildings, but where the artist sat are now homes. In the distance lies the Arabic village of Silwan. One can take pleasant walks through this peaceful valley, just outside the walls of Jerusalem.

You stored up water in the Lower Pool. You built a reservoir between the two walls for the water of the Old Pool.

—Isaiah 22:9, 11

Here lies the Dead Sea, seen from the desolation of the Judean desert. On the other side are the mountains of the country that is called "Moab" in the Bible. The Dead Sea has an overall length of 45 miles and is nowhere wider than 9 miles. No living creature shows itself near the Dead Sea but scientists have nevertheless discovered many microorganisms in the water. The water has healing powers, and Herod the Great came here to take a cure in the salt water and the mineral springs.

In the foreground is the monastery of St. Saba and today there is yet another monastery near the Dead Sea—the monastery of Qumran. It was in this region the Dead Sea Scrolls were discovered, among them the famous Isaiah Scroll. This scroll provides important proof for the historical reliability of the Bible.

The grass withers and the flowers fall, but the word of our God stands forever.

—Isaiah 40:8

36 ANCIENT JEZREEL

In the drawing we see an Arabian village, now called Zarian, where once the ancient city of Jezreel stood. That was the city where the notorious King Ahab had his winter palace when it became too cold on the hill on which Samaria was built—property he acquired by having its owner, Naboth, stoned. Here the brook Kidron enters the plain of Jezreel. It is a large, fertile plain that was considered "the granery of Palestine" and is in our day once again a flourishing agricultural region. But from the Bible this plain is primarily known as a battlefield and will be, according to God's Word, the scene of the final battle between God and the nations.

"In that day I will respond," declares the Lord—"I will respond to the skies, and they will respond to the earth; and the earth will respond to the grain, the new wine and oil, and they will respond to Jezreel."
—Hosea 2:21–22

37 BETHLEHEM

Bethlehem lies only 6 miles south of Jerusalem. The name means "house of bread" because of the fertile farmland in the area, which provides such a sharp contrast with the desert of Judah, vaguely seen in the background. The city is built on two hills, at 2549 feet elevation. Its population now numbers about 30,000, most of whom are Christians.

The city is full of biblical memories. It is the native city of David, who as a boy wandered through these fields. But it is especially the place where Jesus Christ was born, as the prophet Micah predicted. Roberts' drawing reflects the biblical atmosphere better than modern Bethlehem does.

But you, Bethlehem Ephrathah, though you are small among the clans of Judah, out of you will come for me one who will be ruler over Israel.

—Micah 5:2

ASHKELON OF THE PHILISTINES

Here we see the ruins of Ashkelon, where in the first part of the last century the foundations of a large fortification and of a Christian church had been discovered. Solid sections of the ancient city walls are still standing today in a well-designed national park. In the Philistine ruins many wine cups and beer jugs have been found. The Philistines drank a great deal and held large festivals. Another specialty of theirs was the melting and forging of iron, which they must have learned from the Hittites in Asia Minor, perhaps on their way to Canaan. The iron weapons gave them supremacy for a long period of time but they did not escape the prophecy of God's judgment.

Gaza will be abandoned and Ashkelon left in ruins. The word of the LORD is against you, O Canaan, land of the Philistines. "I will destroy you, and none will be left."
—**Zephaniah 2:4–5**

39 THE GRAVE OF ZECHARIAH

At the foot of the Mount of Olives, in the Valley of Jehoshaphat, this beautiful monument has been carved in the rock. The artist found the architectural style attractive because of its mixture of Greek beauty and Egyptian forcefulness. This monument can still be found today, almost exactly as Roberts saw it, on a walk through the picturesque valley, where automobiles are not able to come. It lies near the monument of Absalom (see picture 24) and is easily recognizable from a great distance from all directions.

The prophet Zechariah prophesied about 500 B.C. He helped with the rebuilding of the temple after the return from the Babylonian captivity. He has been called "the prophet of the advent" because he announced the coming of the Messiah. His breathtaking visions speak of this coming.

> *Rejoice greatly, O Daughter of Zion! Shout, Daughter of Jerusalem! See, your king comes to you, righteous and having salvation, gentle and riding on a donkey, on a colt, the foal of a donkey.*
> —Zechariah 9:9

"When we approached the river, everyone began to run and the women uttered excited exclamations. Even the heavily laden camels could not be restrained. A young Greek was dragged down to the stream and drowned before our eyes. Young and old, man and woman, were soon in the stream, one large mass. Some even risked drowning."

"Jordan" means "descending stream." The river, 210 miles long, originates at the foot of Mount Hermon, follows a winding course, and ends in the Dead Sea after a total drop of no less than 2953 feet. It is not difficult to understand that this river has always strongly appealed to the imagination, because John the Baptist baptized here, and because Jesus was baptized here.

Then Jesus came from Galilee to the Jordan to be baptized by John. As soon as Jesus was baptized, he went up out of the water.
—Matthew 3:13, 16

Banks of the Jordan April 2nd 1839.

41 TYRE

In modern Lebanon one looks in vain for signs reading "Tyre," but the city is now called Sur, the ancient Phoenician name that means "Rock." The city is indeed a rock in the sea; it once was an island, but is now a peninsula. Alexander the Great could take the fortified city only after building a dam, which has remained ever since, and can clearly be seen here. Because part of the city was built on the coast, Tyre has actually become a twin city, connected by an isthmus. The population numbers about 5,000 and contains mostly Muslims. It is an out-of-the-way town, without good connections, near the Israeli border. Jesus spoke of this city when He told the Jewish cities that they were more wicked than the pagan cities of Phoenicia.

> *Woe to you, Korazin! Woe to you, Bethsaida! If the miracles that they performed in you had been performed in Tyre and Sidon, they would have repented long ago in sackcloth and ashes. But I tell you, it will be more bearable for Tyre and Sidon on the day of judgment than for you.*
>
> **—Matthew 11:20–21**

THE CHURCH OF JOHN THE BAPTIST

Here we see again a pastoral scene at the foot of the mountain on which Samaria was built. From this side we see the still imposing pillars of a Christian church that was named after John the Baptist. There were even two churches dedicated to him, one dating from the fourth century, the other from the sixth. The graves of Obadiah, Elisha, and John the Baptist were venerated here. When Matthew speaks of the death of John the Baptist on Herod's birthday he does not indicate where this happened. But Samaria (Sebaste) was rebuilt by Herod, so there was a connection. Tradition claims that he was incarcerated, tortured, and decapitated in Sebaste, but his head is also venerated in Constantinople and in Damascus. Therefore we cannot say anything definite about it, although we cannot exclude the possibility that his followers prepared a final resting place for him here in Samaria.

Now Herod had arrested John and bound him and put him in prison. The king . . . had John beheaded in the prison. John's disciples came and took his body and buried it.
—Matthew 14:3, 9, 11, 13

Ruins of the Church of St. John, Sebaste.

Roberts here once again had the opportunity to indulge in his love for the pomp and circumstance of the ancient oriental costumes. He has added some force by drawing the people in various states of worship or ecstasy, or by drawing them singing or reading from books. In the center we see a large slab of polished marble that covers the actual stone where the body of Jesus was laid after Joseph of Arimathea had obtained permission to take care of the body: "The stone of anointing." The grave of this Joseph is also pointed out here in a small, dark room. There is also the "Chapel of the Angel," and there another stone is revered, the stone that is supposed to have closed off the entrance to the grave and that was rolled away by the angel.

As evening approached, there came a rich man from Arimathea, named Joseph, who had himself become a disciple of Jesus. Joseph took the body, wrapped it in a clean linen cloth, and placed it in his own tomb that he had cut out of the rock.
—Matthew 27:57, 59–60

Stone of Unction.
Holy Sepulchre.

44 THE GOLDEN GATE

The walls of Jerusalem are still impressive. Jesus' disciples were as impressed with the walls 2,000 years ago as are today's tourists from all over the world. The Golden Gate is in the eastern wall of the city, and gave access to the temple yard. It is a double gate; one arch symbolizes penance, and the other mercy. According to Arabic writers the Golden Gate was bricked up permanently in 1945, perhaps out of fear from enemy attack.

As he was leaving the temple, one of his disciples said to him, "Look, Teacher! What massive stones! What magnificent buildings!"
—Mark 13:1

Golden Gate of the Temple
Shewing part of the ancient walls

45 ON GOLGOTHA

The Church of the Holy Sepulcher covers not only the place of Jesus' grave, but also Golgotha, the hill where the execution by crucifixion took place. This Hebrew name has been latinized to "Calvary," which contains the word for "skull," hence "Place of the Skull." It has been thought that this hill had the shape of a skull, although other explanations have also been given.

The grave lies in this chapel, a high, large dome, the Rotunda, covered with marble and containing many lamps, candles, and paintings. A worn staircase leads down to a grave six feet wide, that is cut into the rock. In those days most graves were family graves, but this is a grave for one person.

They brought Jesus to the place called Golgotha (which means the Place of the Skull).
—Mark 15:22

RAMLA, THE ANCIENT ARIMATHEA

The city of Ramla lies near Lod, the international airport of Israel. The large tower (98 feet high) still stands. It was built in the fourteenth century by Muslims as the minaret of a large mosque. The builders took into consideration that it also had to serve as a watchtower, and today's visitors can still enjoy daily the view from the platform, if they do not mind climbing the circular staircase of 119 steps! In the drawing a church is clearly visible; a church apparently did stand here, although today only the ruins of a caravansery can be seen with large subterranean vaults, the water reservoirs. The city we see here was founded in A.D. 716 by the Arabs, but it is possible that this is also the site of the ancient Arimathea. A monastery in the main street is called "The Hospice of St. Nicodemus and St. Joseph of Arimathea."

Joseph of Arimathea, a prominent member of the Council, who was himself waiting for the kingdom of God, went boldly to Pilate and asked for Jesus' body.

—Mark 15:43

47 THE CHURCH OF THE ANNUNCIATION

This church wants to remind us of the Annunciation and we should forget all the legends and stories that have later been woven around it. The church visited by Roberts was built in 1730 by the Franciscans on the foundations of a crusader church and was torn down in 1955. In 1969 a new church was completed, rather massive, with a large dome, and a large mosaic behind the altar depicting the church universal. There is a cave where the angel is supposed to have appeared to Mary. Like many sacred places, it all makes a forceful impression.

But the angel said to her, "Do not be afraid, Mary, you have found favor with God. You will be with child and give birth to a son, and you are to give him the name Jesus."
—Luke 1:30–31

Shrine of the Annunciation, Nazareth. April 20th 1839

THE GROTTO OF THE NATIVITY IN BETHLEHEM

Hic de Virgine Maria Jesus Christus Natus est: Here Jesus Christ was born of the Virgin Mary. This is the inscription in the grotto where the birth of Jesus probably took place. It is well possible that the stable of the inn at Bethlehem was a grotto like this one. The exact place where Mary gave birth to her firstborn is said to be the shallow depression to the left, in which fifteen lamps hang, donated by fifteen different Christian groups or churches. A silver star is inlaid in the marble floor to indicate the spot even more precisely. On the paintings above it we see the three magi kneel before mother and child.

While they were there, the time came for the baby to be born, and she gave birth to her firstborn, a son. She wrapped him in strips of cloth and placed him in a manger, because there was no room for them in the inn.

—Luke 2:6–7

Shrine of the Nativity,
Bethlehem April 6th 1839

THE CHURCH OF THE NATIVITY IN BETHLEHEM

The Church of the Nativity is like a citadel built over the grotto where Jesus is supposed to have been born. One enters through a low opening; the main entrance was bricked in long ago to prevent its collapse. Four rows of reddish pillars support the roof and, as the drawing shows, are decorated by representations of biblical saints. The cornice of the pillars was once richly decorated with mosaics and Greek inscriptions from the twelfth century, but today only portions remain. In the floor a mosaic has been found with the Greek word for "fish," *ichthus*; the letters of this word are the opening letters of the Greek words for "Jesus Christ, Son of God, Savior."

"Do not be afraid. I bring you good news of great joy that will be for all the people. Today in the town of David a Savior has been born to you; he is Christ the Lord."
—Luke 2:10–11

50 NAZARETH

When Jesus lived there, Nazareth was an insignificant village. There was a proverb at this time, "Can anything good come from Nazareth?" History has answered that question. The name of this village has become known and loved throughout the world as the native town of "Jesus of Nazareth," and it was here His father worked as a carpenter—and where Jesus also learned the trade. The city lies here peacefully among the hills, but we know from the Gospels that the population could sometimes become vicious quickly. The Nazarites tried to throw Jesus from a precipice after He had spoken in their synagogue and revealed Himself as the promised Messiah. The attitude of the people of Nazareth today toward Jesus is very different; most are Arabic Christians, and it is a city full of monasteries, churches, and chapels, and of course is filled with tourists.

Jesus went to Nazareth, where he had been brought up, and on the Sabbath day he went into the synagogue, as was his custom. All the people in the synagogue were furious when they heard this. They got up, drove him out of the town, and took him to the brow of the hill on which the town was built, in order to throw him down the cliff.
—Luke 4:16, 28–29

51

According to the monks of this monastery, this is the place where Jesus was almost thrown down by the enraged population of Nazareth. However, this seems unlikely because that mountain lay almost two miles outside the city. Roberts says, "An enraged public is not likely to go such a long way, when they could have thrown Jesus over a cliff almost anywhere."

This monastery was founded in 1620 and built on the edge of the cliff. And because the medieval monks were only moderately impressed with the story as found in Luke 4, they embellished it with a number of inventive details. They still say that Jesus saved Himself by jumping down, rather than by walking through the crowd, as the Gospel records.

All the people in the synagogue were furious when they heard this. They got up, drove him out of the town, and took him to the brow of the hill on which the town was built, in order to throw him down the cliff. But he walked right through the crowd and went on his way.

—Luke 4:28–30

52

THE SEA OF GALILEE

The modern name Yam Kinneret comes right from the Old Testament; it is the name translated in the Bible as "Sea of Gennesaret." The name indicates that the sea is shaped like a harp. More common names are "Sea of Galilee" or "Sea of Tiberias." It is 13 miles long, and 7 miles at its widest point; it reaches a depth of some 164 feet. Its level is 689 feet below that of the Mediterranean. Its low elevation is the reason it is often very warm by this sea.

In the foreground we see the town of Tiberias and in the background Mount Hermon with its snow-capped peaks, 9232 feet high. In Jesus' time it was a densely populated region with many settlements along the shores and hundreds of ships on the sea. Here Jesus called the disciples; young fishermen became from that time on fishers of men. On the northwestern shore was Capernaum, where Jesus lived.

One day as Jesus was standing by the Lake of Gennesaret . . . he saw at the water's edge two boats, left there by the fishermen. Then Jesus said, "Don't be afraid; from now on you will catch men." So they pulled their boats up to shore, left everything and followed him.
—Luke 5:1–2, 11

Modern Saida, the ancient Sidon, is a city south of Beirut in Lebanon, on the Mediterranean coast. Walking along the quay where a few small fishing boats bob up and down, it is impossible to imagine that once large fleets of warships came and went here. But today no reminder of the past can be found in this city of about 45,000. The city is mentioned as early as in the Book of Genesis and in many other books of the Old Testament, but also in Homer. It has been destroyed many times but each time it was rebuilt. It flourished briefly in the sixteenth century, but was later overshadowed by Beirut.

Both Tyre and Sidon, which are often mentioned in one breath, were warned many times by the prophets because of their sinfulness. But later the inhabitants of these cities traveled far to hear Jesus and to be healed of their illnesses and unclean spirits. Jesus once withdrew here and Paul visited the city.

He went down with them and stood on a level place. A large crowd of his disciples was there and a great number of people from all over Judea, from Jerusalem, and from the seacoast of Tyre and Sidon, who had come to hear him and to be healed of their diseases.
—Luke 6:17–18

SIDON, Looking towards Lebanon

"It was unforgettable what we saw when we descended from the mountains. The valley lay before us in all the beauty of an oriental evening. The Dead Sea, the silver ribbon of the swift Jordan, could still just be seen, the colors of the pilgrims' camp sparkled in the last rays of the sun; all these were more suitable for the poet than for the painter. The pencil cannot reproduce it." Thus the artist enjoyed the descent from the mountains of Judah to the lowest and hottest place on earth near the Dead Sea. From the plateau of Jerusalem one descends to 1309 feet below sea level, while the sea itself is another 1420 feet deep.

These mountains were notorious in biblical times because of the bandits who lived there. We can't help but think of the Parable of the Good Samaritan, in which a traveler is attacked and left half-dead. In the Red Pass, so called because of the reddish color of the soil, we can still find remnants of what was called "The Inn of the Good Samaritan." This area is now a part of the West Bank.

A man was going down from Jerusalem to Jericho, when he fell into the hands of robbers. They stripped him of his clothes, beat him and went away, leaving him half dead.
—Luke 10:30

55

THE CHAPEL OF ST. HELENA

The most incredible legends have sprung up around the cross and grave of Jesus. His death and the grave provide a more fertile ground in this respect than the Resurrection. Thus there is the story of Helena, the mother of the first Christian emperor of Rome, Constantine. In 326 she visited the holy city of Jerusalem, and was led by divine inspiration to this place, where she discovered the cross of Jesus, as well as the crosses of the criminals who were crucified with Him. One wonders how she could tell these crosses apart. The answer is quite simple: a critically ill woman was instantaneously healed when she touched the right cross!

The legends are not entirely without value, because they do point to the historicity of this place, which scholars also support. Excavations have brought to light several tombstones that indicate that there was indeed a cemetery here.

Two other men, both criminals, were also led out with him to be executed. When they came to the place called The Skull, there they crucified him, along with the criminals—one on his right, the other on his left.

—Luke 23:32–33

CRYPT of the Holy Sepulchre, Jerusalem

56

THE CHURCH OF THE HOLY SEPULCHER

The church stands on the place where already in very early times the grave of Jesus was believed to be. The present basilica was built by the crusaders on the foundations of a church built during the time of Emperor Constantine. Directly underneath the dome can be seen the sepulcher itself. The structures have been repeatedly altered and expanded over the centuries, so that it has become a conglomerate of chapels.

The location is fairly reliable, for places of burial used to lie outside the city walls, as is true of this place. Emperor Hadrian built a pagan temple here in an attempt to eradicate the memory of Jesus, but by doing so he drew attention to the place. It remains a strange experience to see the sepulcher of Jesus revered to this extent since He rose from the dead.

He is not here; he has risen!
—**Luke 24:6**

Church of the Holy Sepulchre
Jerusalem

57

THE WELL OF CANA

At the wedding at Cana Jesus changed water into wine. And that water came from this well, which still provides remarkably pure water. This must be the true well, since it is the only one in the area. It is no longer found in the open field, but inside the Franciscan church, and over the entrance to the church are the words "We worship the place where His feet stood."

In the drawing we see a beautifully decorated sarcophagus that served as a watering trough for the animals. That is not uncommon in the ancient cities of the Near East. Roberts mentions that the Christian pilgrims drink here before visiting Cana.

Nearby stood six stone water jars, the kind used by the Jews for ceremonial washing, each holding from twenty to thirty gallons. Jesus said to the servants, "Fill the jars with water"; so they filled them to the brim.

—John 2:6–7

Fountain at Cana. April 21st 1839.

How beautiful is the landscape of Galilee in the late light of the setting sun! We see here a small caravan and in the distance, 4 miles away, is Cana, the modern Arabian Kfar-Kana.

Two churches can be seen in Cana. The Greek church stands close to the main road, and the priest there shows the "original" jar that was used at the famous wedding in Cana, where Jesus changed the water into wine. The church of the Franciscans stands in the center of the village. A third sanctuary, the chapel of Nathanael, is built, according to tradition, where his house once stood. But apart from these structures Cana is a beautifully situated town that evokes biblical images.

Jesus said to the servants, "Fill the jars with water." They did so, and the master of the banquet tasted the water that had been turned into wine. This, the first of the miraculous signs, Jesus performed in Cana of Galilee.

—John 2:7–9, 11

59

THE SPRING (WELL) OF JACOB IN SHECHEM

East of the city of Nablus lies the biblical Shechem or Sychar, now called Askar. There Roberts found only a few steps of a stone staircase, the remnants of a church built by the crusaders. Now the solid walls of a monastic church, laid out in the shape of a cross, but never finished, occupy the site; the structure does not have a roof.

Roberts meditated: "Here sat the Redeemer, tired of the journey, near the spring and taught the Samaritan woman the great truths that have broken down the walls dividing Jews and Gentiles."

Now he had to go through Samaria. So he came to a town in Samaria called Sychar, near the plot of ground Jacob had given to his son Joseph. Jacob's well was there, and Jesus, tired as he was from the journey, sat down by the well.
—**John 4:4–6**

60

THE POOL OF BETHESDA

The location of this ancient pool is near the Church of St. Anna (compare this drawing with picture 5). The name means "House of Mercy," and the biblical story indicates the reason for this name. From time to time new water with curative properties would well up out of the spring, and it was effective only until it had been absorbed by the standing water, so that the sufferers had to hurry when the water began to move. It is entirely possible that this is indeed the historical Pool of Bethesda, although there were certainly other pools in the ancient city.

Now there is in Jerusalem near the Sheep Gate a pool, which in Aramaic is called Bethesda. Here a great number of disabled people used to lie.

—John 5:2–3

"Through a beautiful landscape we arrived at the Sea of Tiberias, embedded in the surrounding hills. In the distance lay Mount Hermon, covered with snow, and on a nearby hill we saw the city of Safed. Here before us lay the scene of the miracles of our Savior. But the population and the ships were gone. In the west we saw the Jordan flow away in the direction of the Dead Sea, and below us was Tiberias."

Tiberias is the capital of Galilee; only Jews live here. The city is about 2,000 years old and is named after the Roman emperor Tiberias, so in Jesus' day it was an entirely new city.

Some time after this, Jesus crossed to the far shore of the Sea of Galilee (that is, the Sea of Tiberias). Then Jesus went up on the hillside and sat down with his disciples.
—John 6:1, 3

62 THE TOWER OF DAVID

Every ancient Near Eastern city had a citadel, stronghold, or fortress. This citadel in Jerusalem is located in the northwestern part of the city, just south of the Jaffa Gate. It has solid, high walls on top of the rock, and when the crusaders captured Jerusalem in 1099 they had much trouble with the citadel. The oldest portion of the northeast tower or Tower of David, shown here, dates perhaps from the beginning of our era. There were originally three towers.

The grave of David attracts many visitors. It contains a stone sarcophagus, with the silver crowns of the Torah on top. The medieval structure has a second story and tradition claims that Jesus celebrated the Last Supper here with His disciples. To the Christian this is a beautiful thought, because Jesus is also called "the Son of David."

Does not the Scripture say that the Christ will come from David's family and from Bethlehem, the town where David lived?
—John 7:42

63

THE POOL OF SILOAM

The pool of Siloam was a well-known pool inside the walls of Jerusalem in the southern and most vulnerable part of the city. Water was brought here via a tunnel cut through the rock, under the wall to the spring Gihon outside. King Hezekiah had built the tunnel, and in 1880 an inscription was accidentally discovered by some boys playing in the tunnel. The inscription states that the workers who dug the tunnel started from both ends and finally came close enough to be able to hear the other's knock. The water runs over a distance of 1749 feet, and it is possible to walk through the tunnel, wading through waist-deep water.

In this drawing we see the entrance, where 34 steps lead down to the water. The name of the spring, Gihon, means "to flow." And the water has been running here for 2700 years.

"Go," he told him, "wash in the pool of Siloam" (this word means Sent). So the man went and washed, and came home seeing.

—John 9:7

Fountain of Siloam
Valley of Jehoshaphat.

64

THE VILLAGE OF BETHANY

The village of Bethany lies near Jerusalem, on the other side of the Mount of Olives. Its Arabic name is El-Azarja, in which we can hear the name Lazarus, a friend of Jesus, who lived with his sisters Mary and Martha here in Bethany.

A large "Church of Lazarus" stands in Bethany today. Over the altar is found the words Jesus spoke in this village at Lazarus' grave: I am the Resurrection and the Life. A mural depicts the scene John describes in John 11.

"I am the resurrection and the life. He who believes in me will live, even though he dies; and whoever lives and believes in me will never die."

—John 11:25—26

65

INSIDE THE CHURCH OF THE HOLY SEPULCHER

David Roberts was much impressed by the colorful robes he saw inside the church of the Holy Sepulcher in Jerusalem. He visited the church on Palm Sunday, 1839, which marks the beginning of a week of processions and ceremonies in commemoration of the death and burial of Jesus.

Here we see the bishop of the Armenian Christians seated on the throne before the altar. There are also Coptic and Syrian Christians present, because at that time they were too few in number to have their own ceremonies. Roberts thus has drawn not merely a variety of robes, but a real worship service with all its splendor and magnificence.

Carrying his own cross, he went out to The Place of the Skull (which in Aramaic is called Golgotha). Here they crucified him, and with him two others—one on each side and Jesus in the middle.

—John 19:17–18

66 THE DAMASCUS GATE

The Damascus Gate is so-called because it stands at the beginning of the road that leads north to Syria. The Hebrew name is Shechem Gate, because the road also leads to Shechem (Nablus). At the foot of this gate remnants of the walls and the gate from the second century have been excavated. Where the camels stand in the drawing is now a parking lot. On the right we see a few grave markers, which have now given way to a parking area along the wall. In many places outside the city walls there are still graves of Jews, Christians, and Muslims. They were buried here because they expected the Resurrection and judgment to take place here, and they wanted to experience it first.

Through this gate Saul left for Damascus and returned as Paul. It was on this road he received the command to no longer persecute the followers of Jesus, but to follow Him himself.

Meanwhile, Saul was still breathing out murderous threats against the Lord's disciples. He went to the high priest and asked him for letters to the synagogues in Damascus, so that if he found any there who belonged to the Way, whether men or women, he might take them as prisoners to Jerusalem.

—Acts 9:1–2

67 ACRE

This ancient port dates from the time of the Canaanites and was called Acco. Because of its strategic importance the city has been beseiged many times, by the Assyrians, the Egyptians, the Saracens, the crusaders, and later by the Turks, the Arabs, and even by Napoleon, and finally by the British.

It is a tourist attraction today, because the entire city is a virtual open-air museum. In the old section live almost exclusively Arabs (8,000), while the Israelis (24,000) live in the new part of the city. In New Testament times the city was called Ptolemais (after the ruler of Egypt who rebuilt the city). Paul landed here after his third missionary journey and visited the local church.

We continued our voyage from Tyre and landed at Ptolemais, where we greeted the brothers and stayed with them for a day.

—Acts 21:7

PANORAMA OF JERUSALEM

At the end of our journey through the lands of the Bible we take one last look back at Jerusalem. From the road to Bethany we see the holy city, built on many hills. In the center of Mount Moriah stands the Omar Mosque, and to its left the El Aksa Mosque. Somewhat higher to the left lies Mount Zion with the city of David, the Citadel. In the foreground is the valley where the Kidron flows; the curious tower of the memorial of Absalom stands there. Nearby pilgrims kneel down to pray, facing Jerusalem, the holy city of Jews, Christians, and Muslims.

This drawing was made from the Mount of Olives where Jesus often came to pray. From here He left for His last entrance into Jerusalem; from here He ascended and will return to establish the new Jerusalem.

I saw the Holy City, the New Jerusalem, coming down out of heaven from God, prepared as a bride beautifully dressed for her husband.
—Revelation 21:2